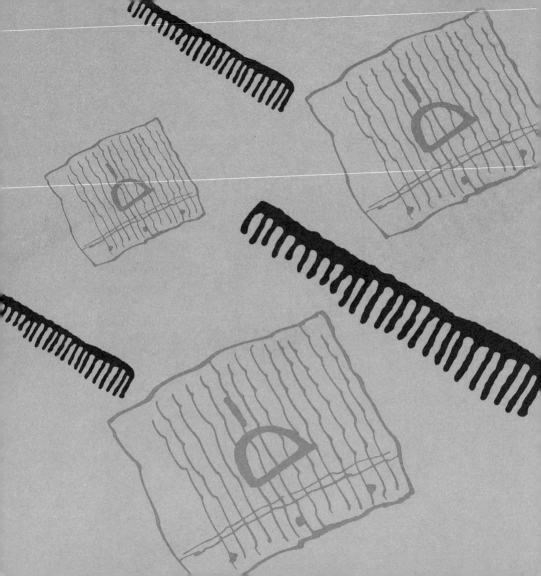

Life Is Like A Ten-Speed Bicycle

by

SCHULZ

KONECKY&KONECKY

Konecky & Konecky LLC
72 Ayers Point Road
Old Saybrook, CT 06475
www.koneckyandkonecky.com

ISBN: 1-56852-768-3

Printed and bound in Hong Kong

Me, Stressed Out?

Your Hair Is The First To Know

I HAVE A THEORY, MARCIE..

I THINK YOUR WHOLE BODY BECOMES SUSPICIOUS WHEN YOU'RE NOT READY FOR A TEST..

AND WHEN YOU LOOK AT THE QUESTIONS...

Life Can
Be A
Stress Test

TRY TO GET THE BALL OVER THE PLATE! YOU THINK WE'RE OUT HERE FOR THE FUN OF IT?!

Things
Could Be
Worse

What's Life Without Worries?

Life Is Like A Ten-Speed Bicycle

Life
Is Full Of
Choices

Life Is Full Of Choices

Searching
For The Meaning
Of Life

Blanket
Wisdom